RAI

PLEASE SEND

MORE RAIN

Please Send More Rain

ISBN: 0692982035
ISBN: 978-0692982037

Cover & interior design by Imani Carter

This book is dedicated to my best friend;
my wonderful husband John.

March 26, 2013

I wouldn't even know where to begin-
Pen to paper
It was all gone
The creative juices that used to flow
ALL GONE
But this is for you
The one who inspired me
I write
For you.

I would like to acknowledge...

My Lord and Savior Jesus Christ who has lavished me with grace, upon grace, upon grace, and lovingly walks with me along my journey in discovering more of His light, joy, and wonder in this beautiful life He has called me to lead.

My amazing, intelligent, and handsome husband John who is my best friend; who loves me unconditionally, sharpens me, and encourages me in my relationship with God and my writing.

My family: My parents- Gwen and Claude, my dad- Jeff, my in-laws- John and Kim, my sisters- Chanele, Cherese, Jade, and Kayla, my brothers- Chris, Jason, and Kendall, my nieces and nephews- Reign, Mariah, and Caleb, and the rest of my family who all motivate me to be a light in this world.

My best friends Imani and Castel who have been my confidants since our first year at Hampton University; who inspire me with their gifts and passions, and who have helped me edit this book.

My gracious pastors Barbara and Baron Brown, and my family at River of Life Worship Center, where I learned to accept the gift of the Holy Spirit, having the space to truly encounter God through worship, all allowing me to grow in my faith.

Minister Caleb and Dr. Phyllis for helping me edit this book; Kim Freeman Brown who wrote the forward; Dr. Minister Karen who told me I need to write a book; and Leilani who pushed me to finish writing.

And Kassie, who met me one time before inviting me to a birthday dinner with a group of young people living bravely for Christ, and helped introduce me to the best adventure I could have ever imagined as a young adult seeking God with all my heart.

Thank you.

CONTENTS

FORWARD

Come Near to God:
The Path to Personal Revival

"O God, You are my God; I shall seek You earnestly;
My soul thirsts for You, my flesh yearns for You, in a
dry and weary land where there is no water."
-Psalm 63:1 (NASB)

Why am I unsatisfied, even after landing my dream job? Why aren't my friends, new clothes and boyfriend enough to make me happy? Why am I so stressed out, depressed, sick and tired even though I'm trying to live my best life like Oprah says I should?

I must have asked myself these questions a million times as a young adult. And I wish I could say that my inquiry led to good choices. It didn't. Instead, I tried to fill my emptiness with things, people, experiences and a few really bad self-help books that only made me feel more unsatisfied and terrified that I'd never truly be happy.

Sound familiar? Most of us at one point in our lives recognize that we hunger and thirst for something we just can't put our finger on, let alone obtain. But this revelation doesn't always lead us to an understanding that what we thirst for is something the world can't provide.

What we long for is a bond with the One who created us. What we all truly desire is a relationship with God.

Please Send More Rain is a powerful testimony and a wonderful demonstration of one young woman's journey to pursue an intimate relationship with God and glorify Him. Raine Brandon's poems paint a beautiful picture of what it looks like, sounds like and feels like to live, move and have our being in the full knowledge of who we are and why we're placed on the planet. Raine's spiritual walk fully responds to God's call in Isaiah 43:7 (NLT) which says, *Bring all whom claim me as their God, for I have made them for my glory. It was I who created them.*

Please Send More Rain is also a fervent, perfect prayer for all of us to experience what happens when God sends rain. Isaiah 44:3 (NIV) reveals God's promise to send rain as an outpouring of His Spirit and blessings on generations to come. *For I will pour water on the thirsty land, and streams on the dry ground; I will pour out my Spirit on your offspring, and my blessing on your descendants.* And James 5:18 (ESV) reveals the outcomes of God's rain when it recounts that *heaven gave rain, and the earth bore its fruit.*

In reading this heartwarming book, see Raine's journey as an inspiration, not a blueprint. The poems within these pages are how she connects with and lives out her purpose. Your path is likely different. God wants to experience the most authentic way you express your worship and praise for Him. He's not looking for perfection. He seeks your genuine heart—no matter how flawed or inadequate you think you are.

Let Him in and watch Him revive the dry and desolate places in your life. As is written in James 4:8 (NIV), *Come near to God and he will come near to you.* Pursuing a personal relationship with God is the path to personal revival of your joy, wholeness, freedom from fear and excitement about your future.

How do I know? Because the moment I began investing more time in knowing God, I no longer asked the questions I once did. My favorite scripture, Psalms 37:4 (ESV), is my testimony. *Delight yourself in the Lord and he will give you the desires of your heart.* The blessings that come when you focus first on God are bigger and better than what you could ever dream for yourself.

I stand in agreement with Raine's prayer that God sends rain to quench the thirst of His people. Please send the reviving rain, Lord, and set us all on a path of purpose that is aligned with Your perfect will. To God Be The Glory.

-Kimberly Freeman Brown
Author of *And Still I Rise: Black Women Labor Leader's Voices|Power|Promise*, and *I Dream Detroit: The Voice and Vision of Women of Color on Detroit's Future*

INTRODUCTION

The Heart of a Writer: My Journey

When I was a little girl it was my heart's desire to grow up and become a writer. I would create stories and write poetry constantly. I have also been journaling consistently since I was twelve years old. Writing was a way for me to express everything I was feeling inside of me- the good, the bad, and everything in between. Little did I know, writing would become my primary way of communicating with God.

Prior to knowing the power of prayer or what it meant to worship God, writing was like talking to a best friend who didn't speak to me audibly, but is always there and who I see and feel through the pages. Even before I truly understood the influence of writing in my life, the Holy Spirit spoke to me through my words and guided me along a path that He had already paved the way for me, but gave me the grace to choose it for myself.

Somewhere along the way, my childhood dreams of becoming a writer went away. I didn't major in English in college, but went on to become a social worker. I still loved writing, but I wanted to keep it for myself. I never imagined that I would be a published author at 27. I never thought that I would share my personal, intimate, vulnerable words with others, until the day things began to change for me.

It was during the summer of 2014, I had just returned from a mission's trip to Belize with nine other young people from my church and was volun-told that I would be sharing a poem at our upcoming young adult conference. I was being called to step from behind the curtain, the background where I preferred to be, where

I was comfortable, and onto the stage where my light could shine for all the world to see. Or in this case, my church's congregation.

This became my first time ever sharing my poetry in a public setting, on a stage in front of a large group of people. I was terrified. The poem that I chose to perform was an expression of the place where I go in my head to meet with my Father in heaven and spend time with Him. He helped me write that piece, and He gave me the boldness to share it.

Since then I have been writing and sharing my poetry with a fire and boldness I never knew was within me. I still get scared. When people read or hear my poetry I never know if they are going to like it or hate it, if they think it's childish or brilliant, or if they think I should just keep my thoughts to myself. Then that one person comes up to me and tells me how they admire my bravery and how my words touched them, or how they relate to what I shared. That one person reassures me enough for me to do it again.

I've realized that the creative gifts God has graced me with are first for Him, to be a testament of His glory, and then for the world. I can't allow fear, rejection, doubt, or anything else that may hold us back from chasing after our dreams to keep me from sharing His love with the world. There is no fear in love and I truly believe that, just like I believe in the One who crafted me in His image.

This book isn't meant to have you believe what I believe, but my hope is that it will encourage you to be who you were created to be, inspire you to chase after your own dreams, and challenge you to do some self-reflection. I'm sharing a piece of myself, what's on my heart so that maybe, just maybe, I can reach that one person who says, "I understand and I want more."

I know what it feels like to desire more in life. I know what it's like to sense that there is something missing. And I know how it is to be scared of letting go. Over the past five years I have been on a journey of deeper intimacy in my relationship with the Holy Spirit. He has broken down my walls, helping me to forgive others, as well as myself, just as the Father forgives us. I've learned just how fun living a Christian lifestyle can be; it's true freedom. I have been forced to loosen the grip on the control I thought I had over my life, realizing that His plans for me are far greater and are indeed what my heart desires.

I've experienced His grace that is so awe-filled that I wouldn't be able to thank Him enough for my entire lifetime. My faith is being built up each and everyday, in every area of my life and through everything I encounter. I understand that it's the small things that count that make the big things in life a true miracle.

And love. The Father has loved me my whole life and showed me examples of His love through my parents, family members, friends, teachers, coworkers, and even strangers. And through His Son, Jesus Christ. Yet, it wasn't until I learned how to accept His love that I was able to fully grasp it with my whole heart. I'm still letting go. I'm still learning the intricacies of His deep love for me. I desire to seek Him unceasingly, and I hope that *Please Send More Rain* will move you enough to seek Him too.

Grace & Peace,
Raine K. Brandon

"I lift my hands to you in prayer. I thirst for you as parched land thirsts for rain...."

-Psalms 143:6 (NLT)

PART I

BEFORE THE RAIN BEGAN TO FALL

THE FOUNDATION

I stood still at the top of the mountain,
looking out at the fire that blazed from the forest to the sea.
The smoke emanating from the flames was black.
I yelled at the top of my lungs,
"HE IS GOD!"

A Place Beneath The Stars

let me tell you about my refuge
the place where me
and my Father meet
it is outside our explanation
of time
the place where i worship
at His feet

its beautiful
my refuge
sometimes i close my eyes
and i meet Him there
i dance barefoot
the lush green grass
beneath my feet
dancing under the twilight
only for my Father to see

the air is clean and fresh
mmm not too cold
not too hot
the stars expand forever
and the milky way
bares my reflection

in this space i am free
just me and my Daddy

i dance with my heart
as my body sways
here in this time
when im with Him
i dance the night away
His heart smiles
i praise His name

most times its just
me in this space
as He watches from above
but once with my eyes shut tight
He lay with me in the cool grass
and we gazed at the stars
together
the luminaries twinkled
different shapes and figures
that made us think

then i climbed into His arms
listening to His heart
beat in His chest
it beat like mine

His hands still pierced
the wounds still fresh
why did You do it?
why did You go through
all that pain?

He smiled
and pulled me closer to Him
His touch was indescribable
nothing i had ever felt before
I did it for you baby girl
I did it for this

i cried
please dont ever leave me
He sat us up facing each other
He stared into my soul
and i saw heaven in His eyes
He wiped the tears

from my cheeks
kissed me on my forehead
we will always be
together, My love
until heaven comes
meet Me here
in your refuge
right here in your heart

He ascended back to the stars
i stood up
and continued to dance
for my Father
the lush green grass
beneath my feet
the air clean and fresh
i could feel Him smiling
down at me

its beautiful
my refuge

Grace

Grace that falls like
Rain when it pours
And refreshes my being
Constantly renewing
Everything within me.

Grace that saves my soul
Rendering me helpless
Against the great mercy
Christ bestows upon me
Endlessly.

Grace that shines like light
Radiant and bold
Against the darkness that
Causes us to fall
Every time we draw closer to Him.

Grace flowing like a
River of Life
Awesome and majestic
Cascading through my heart
Eternity in mind.

Grace at the beginning of You
Grace at the end of Me.

Created To Be Like Him

I'm built differently,
with distinctive characteristics and traits.
Special circumstances went into creating me,
from the dust to the womb.
My Father crafted me in His perfection.
I wasn't designed to conform,
and I wasn't birthed to be the same.
I was fashioned to be like His Son.
I am set apart.
There is no one else on this earth like me.
No one in heaven has this spirit in me.
Only my Father,
who calls me beautiful, special, His own.
For years, I attempted to follow the world.
I wanted to fit in-
to be the same as everyone else.
It was like my neurons were wired for me
to be a follower.
But I *am* a follower.
Not of the ways of man,
but of God.
Christ-follower, it's in my name.
Raine Kirstin.
I am a queen
who refreshes and helps make things grow.
See, there was a plan for me.
In my mother's heart
the Holy Spirit placed my name,
and gave me new life through Christ's shed blood.
He redeemed me for my quirkiness
and justified my weirdness.
I guess that's why I will never be able to assimilate
or to fall in line with the status quo.
I wasn't created to,
and neither are you.

In His Wisdom

Stars that shine like the sun reflects on the ocean-
Blinding, yet captivating.

I stand in the middle of everywhere,
gazing up at one of God's first creations-
His majesty in the night sky.
What more do people need to believe in Him?
As hydrogen and helium particles stay afloat
in the sea of the atmosphere.
Above our heads gravity has no hold
on what God has fashioned through His Spirit.
With wisdom as His guide,
faith in the unexplainable.
Scientists try to put reason to everything,
yet God is the only One who knows all things.
He was the beginning,
and He will be the end.

Stop and look up
at the vast splendor of the Aurora Borealis-
Angels dancing in the sky.
The Milky Way, and shooting stars,
all formed to give Him the glory He deserves,
and to satisfy our desire for beauty.
He knows our hearts,
and how stargazing can bring satisfaction,
and delight.

Weightless balls of fire
seamlessly shining brightly
in a sky illuminated by the moon-
Blinding, yet captivating.

The Foundation

He held my hand so gently in His,
as we walked through the field of sunflowers.
The sun shone bright up above,
as the calm wind soothed my anxious soul.
Before our journey, I was terrified
to give my whole self to this Man.
But as we began walking together,
step-by-step, my fear was exchanged for peace.
I felt joy for the first time.
He found me in a place of sadness and hopelessness,
asking me to trust Him and put my faith in Him.
He said that He would carry my burdens,
and ever since, He has.
I've tried to run back-
return to my old comforts that gripped me forcefully.
At times along the way,
I wanted to let go of Him and run away.
But He held on tightly and
wouldn't let me slip from His grasp.
He said He loved me,
but I didn't want to believe Him.
Yet, throughout our time together,
I found that He knows all about me,
more than anyone in my world.
And my heart was opened to receiving His love.
I finally let go of my fears,
and this journey has created a new path in my life.
One where I know I will never be alone again.

Light & Love

I was created by the Master's
hands,
the crafter of the heavens and
earth
whose image is embedded in
mine,
though only some can see His
reflection,
the others are blinded by the
darkness.

I was destined to be Light.
Light like the One
who formed me
in my mother's womb.
Light like the One
who walked the earth
fulfilling His Father's purpose.
Light like Christ who lived,
and died,
and rose for me.
A beautiful rose
and timely resurrection
for a world who was sightless
to His Light,
choosing not to see Him perfect.

But He opened my eyes and
ears,
and healed me
from a life of visionless living,
and deaf loving.
His Word was unveiled to me
and now I finally comprehend
the Love
that was coded in my DNA,
the blood that was shed
on a cross
flows through my veins.

Before I didn't get it-
I didn't understand,
nor did I care to.
I was just like
this fallen creation,
believing I was a good girl,
one who always did
the right thing.
Yet I was born in iniquity.
And that sin I tried to avoid
was still on the edge
of my fingertips,
right on the tip of my tongue
for the father of darkness
to utilize at his every whim.

But Christ came into my life,
and I came into His.
Being born again
into His likeness,
into His saving grace,
His mercy,

Joy!
Peace!

Salvation, redemption,
and justification.

The Spirit called to me
so I could hear Him.
A sweet lullaby
with words and melodies
just for me.
He knew how to get my
attention
and how to draw me closer.
He always knew.

Now I choose
to walk with a purpose,
to walk in the shadow of a King.
He called me to be His heir,
His daughter,
His bride.

My Father's request
is not one
that I would ever deny.
To fulfill His plan for me
is my destiny and heart's desire,
so that not only
will I be with Him in eternity,
basking in the bright brilliance
of His majestic kingdom,
but the lives I touch
with His Love
would also have
the opportunity
to share in *this* hope,
to receive the promises
He gave us
from the beginning of time.

He is the author,
the illustrator,
the master of all.

So although satan thinks
he has his grip on this world,
he is but a serpent on the
ground
whose head will be crushed.

Young people it's our time
to rise up from our slumber.
To no longer succumb
to the temptations of this
domain.
To die daily to ourselves
and be baptized
and made whole
through the power
of the Holy Spirit.
It's time to unify
and come together as one body,
fighting for the praises of
Elohim.
And Love
to be spread across this planet.

It begins in our hearts.
Let Him in
and let Him wash away
all the dirt and grime
that has attached itself to you
so strongly.
Let the Spirit breathe
that newness of life into you

so you don't have to return
to your old ways.
Let us be like Enoch
and walk with Adonai
all the days of our lives,
so that when we finally reach
that Day of Judgment
we can hear Him say,
Friend, I'm glad you're
finally here.
Come and enjoy the lavish feast
I have prepared for you,
you've done well by faith.

Faith!

Let it take control of your mind
so that you will no longer be
lost in your intellect,
lacking awareness
and feeling out of control,
because He is the One
in complete control.
Let the wisdom of Proverbs
fill you and guide you,
giving you the discernment
needed
to stay in Yahweh's will
for your life.

And Love-

Love is patient.
Love is kind.
Love is accepting
His affection for you
so that you may go
into this broken world
and Love others-
Love all.

Let it fill you to overflowing
so that even in hard times,
which there will be,
God's agape Love
still permeates your very soul
and your spirit is connected
with His Spirit,
holy leading you.

I thank Jehovah
for His Holy Spirit
that takes residence
in my limbs,
because the flesh is weak.
And yes I am righteous,
but not perfect.
Perfected through Him
in repentance and sanctification,
everyday seeking to be more
and more like Him.

To walk in holiness.
To be pure.
That is my desire.
That is my desire for you.
To know Him,
and to serve Him,

and to consciously live
a life pleasing to Him.
Not in your own power,
but by the power of God
which is greater than anyone,
or anything, or any god
who may try to deceive you
into believing
that God does not exist.
That He is weak.

Because in the Father's strength
and power,
His wisdom,
He created the heavens
and the earth.
He formed us.
He is the author
and finisher of our faith,
and He will be there in the end
to show you
just how powerful He is.

So no longer believe
in your powerlessness,
because through Him
we are made to be gods.
Not God,
as some would so mistakenly
think.
But gods-
His people,
doing His work
that He started for us
to do here on earth.
Because one day
there will be a new earth
with no darkness,
no need for the moon or night.
We will be crowned in exaltation,
walking on streets of gold
and basking
in colors of the unknown.

One day we will be Light.
We will be Love.
Like He created us,
in His image,
in His likeness,
We will live.

Journal Reflection

In "A Place Beneath The Stars," the author describes her refuge, the place she has imagined in her heart where she meets with God. In her refuge she is free to be herself in the care of her Father. It is where she goes in her prayer time and times of worship. Do you have a refuge, whether it be internal or external? Describe it with as much detail as possible.

Do some research online and in the Bible on the meaning of your name. What does your name mean and how do you think it expresses who God has created you to be?

THE QUESTION

Do you believe?
How do you know?
Do you trust that God is real?
How can you be sure?

You can't give your whole heart
to someone you don't have faith in,
so what are you holding on to?

Doubt

Fear

Control

Let it all go.

Torn: An Ode To Church

Why do I feel so torn between the old, the first,
and the new, which now has become home?
I feel like I shouldn't have these thoughts and emotions.
I should be satisfied right where I am,
here in this place of celebration.

Both offer the love of God that I desire.
The old holds the foundation for my faith,
yet the new embraces opportunity for growth.

I love what I had,
but I want the new more.

Here I…
I know that my dreams will come true.
With the old living inside of me,
and the new growing all around.
To fulfill God's purpose for my life,
and allow His river of life to flow through me
I know this decision is right.

I will step into the new.

Critical Thinking

Genesis inquires so many questions from me.
There are so many events
and people left unexplained
only for my mind to wonder.
Who?
What?
Where?
When?
Why?
Questions that I wish I could know the answers to-
the *mysteries* of God!

I write them down in the margins of my study Bible,
hoping to receive a revelation or a word of knowledge.
Nonetheless, I continue reading,
revelation-less about the questions I have put forth
and more critical thinking ensues.
It's what I have been trained to do
as a worker of the social good,
which I call Christ-work.
Seeing as how He was the best social worker,
people fail to recognize the magnificent career He led.

Which-

Began in Genesis,
where my inquiries arise.
Where He was with God
and through the Holy Spirit
with all wisdom and power
He created the universe
and had Moses author this telling
of the beginning of creation,
learning, himself, the intricacies of our Father.

So I wish to be like Enoch,
and walk with God the rest of my life,
so that I too
would be with Him in the cool of the day,
having my questions answered.

It Is A Choice

He shot me.

Pain.

Doubt.

Fear.

Anger.

Sin.

He shot me.

Everything around me began to spin and then it all went black…

Where am I?

I opened my eyes and I was in a rectangular shaped room draped in white, sitting at a long bronzed wooden table. I sat in the middle. At the far left-hand side, there was a little girl sitting in a chair. She had bright red bows holding her bleached white hair in two ponytails. On the far right-hand side of the table sat a seemingly tall man with dull grey hair. He wore a purple bowtie.

"You have a choice."
The little girl lured.
"Come to me."

I looked down the table at her. She looked so cute.
I began to get out of my chair and walk towards her.

"You have a choice."
The tall man said.
"Choose life."

I turned towards him and saw his hand outstretched towards me.
I began to cry, but I didn't know why.

What is happening to me?
Am I dead?

"Die to yourself."
The man whispered.
"Trust in the One who calls you by name."

"Come have fun with us."
The girl enticed.
"I will give you everything you've ever desired."

My heart's desire?

"Do you desire the things of this broken world,
or do you desire eternity?
Come with me,
and I will give you the life you were created for.
A life in paradise."
The man with the purple bowtie moved closer to me as he spoke. I could see him more clearly now. His grey hair from afar turned out to be beautiful shining silver. Instead of the wrinkles I expected to see, his face was smooth and unblemished. The closer he moved to me I could see that he was strong, fit and young. I was shockingly attracted to him.

"He's lying to you!
Come with me and we can rule the world together."
The little girl began moving closer to me. As she came closer I saw that she was not cute at all, and although she had the voice of a child her appearance was that of an old woman. Her teeth were crooked and her eyes and face splotched with disease. She was terrifying.

They were now both standing next to me on each side.
I felt a shiver run through my spine.

"It's your choice."
The young man professed.

"You know where you want to be."
The scary woman induced.

I was created for eternity?

Yes.

I have made my choice.

I closed my eyes and when they opened again
they were almost blinded by a bright light.

"Forgive me, Father. Forgive me.
I love You and I trust You.
Please don't let me go."

"You had already made your choice a long time ago
when you accepted Me into your heart.
I saved you then, and
I've already covered you with grace.
Yes, you've sinned numerous times, but
you are forgiven.
You are purified and made new by My blood.
The enemy has no hold over you.
He may have shot you,
but he cannot kill you.
You are alive in Me."

Now live.

Serve Me Anyway

I wish I was as receptive as Lydia,
searching for truth
and accepting of Your Word
with enough gratefulness
to share it with others.
But You say,
"You're perfect,
serve me anyway."

I wish I was as bold as Stephen,
spreading Your gospel
on the street corners,
facing the possibility of stoning
or martyrdom,
knowing that saying Your Name
could be my last words.
But You say,
"You're perfect,
serve me anyway."

I wish I was as devoted as
Hannah,
coming to You in prayer
early in the morning
despite what people
may think of me,
and giving my all to You.
But You say,
"You're perfect,
serve me anyway."

I wish I was as faithful as Job
to continue serving You
when the trials come,
and I feel like giving up,
not knowing what tomorrow
may bring.
But You say,
"You're perfect,
serve me anyway."

I wish I was as spiritual
as Elizabeth,
never doubting
Your ability in my life,
knowing that You will
fulfill Your promises,
and I am treasured by You.
But You say,
"You're perfect,
serve me anyway."

I wish I was as prophetic as
Isaiah,
responding to Your call
with, *Here I am, send me,*
telling the world
of Your future coming in glory.
But You say,
"You're perfect,
serve me anyway."

I wish my hair was long
like the woman in Luke,
anointing You with my
jar of alabaster.
As tears stream down my
cheeks,my hair would
wipe them away
as I kiss Your feet.
As everyone around me
shouts out that I am a sinner,
You simply tell me how
I am forgiven.

How I am made whole in You.
How my faith has saved me,
and all that You want from me is
my heart surrendered.

From this moment forward,
I see that You are perfect.
That by giving You
every piece of myself,
I am made perfect in love.
And I will serve You anyway.

The Question

What would it be like to stand on the face of the deep
and watch God's masterful creation
come to life right before your eyes,
beyond the imagination of human capabilities
occurring years upon years
after the children of man began to populate the earth?

Sin grew rampant-
causing the death and destruction of the seed that grew
in iniquity and shaped our history
that rocked the foundations of this planet,
and the core value of love
was still something to be found.

Yet, God
in His supreme love and justice
sovereignly destroyed the human race
leaving one righteous,
one family,
one pair of each animal to save humanity
and give His people another chance
at a life that would lead us into eternity,
into life on a new earth,
with no tears,
with no violence
that was the cause of the flood in the first place.

And no pride that led the people following Nimrod
to think they were God in creating Babel.

And no deceit that led Eve to sin,
and for her husband to follow so unprotesting,
when in fact, he was created to follow Christ so that he could lead.

What would it be like to *lead* like Ezra
and Nehemiah
when the Jews returned home to their promised land
and experienced true revival?

Journal Reflection

Think about any reservations you may have about believing and following God completely. If you have some, what are they? What are you holding onto and how do you think you can let go?

Have there been any hard decisions that you've had to make regarding the direction God was calling you? What was the outcome?

Are there times when you feel inadequate to serve God? How has God shown you that He loves when you come to Him just as you are?

THE CALL

There are words that you need to hear
So listen
Because time is limited
And the words won't be here to save you forever
So listen now
While there is still a chance.

His Proposal

"You are beautiful.
I created you to see
Yourself in Me.

You will live and not die.
Don't doubt Me.
Don't distrust the promises
I have shown you.

She loves you,
Forgive her.

Live your life in the freedom
You have been longing for,
In Me.

Dance.
Be silly.

Share My love with the world.
Don't be ashamed or fearful
Of whom I created you to be.
Share your testimonies.

You are My beloved,
I love you with all My heart.

Your Adam,
He's coming.
I am preparing him
In the secret place
Just as I've kept you hidden.
You search for Me
And he will find you,
And you will know.

Don't be confused.

Let it all go:
The fear
The doubt
The insecurities
The anger
The disbelief
The shame
The lies
The heartbreak
The lust
The relationships
The unforgiveness
The feelings of abandonment
Let it all go, baby girl.

Surrender your heart to Me.
I will cleanse you
And make you pure as snow.
I will wholly restore you
And make you new.

You are passion.
You are peace.
You are wisdom.

I am breaking all of
Those walls down.
Let Me.

They can't hurt you anymore.

And those dreams-
They can't,
They won't hold you back.

I am your peace.
Remember, in times of distress,
I will come to your refuge.
I will meet you
In the quiet of your heart,
And I will comfort you.

Your destiny will be fulfilled
On this earth and in eternity.
Just dance with Me
All the days of your life.
Every day if you do nothing else,
Dance with Me under the stars.

Seek Me
With your whole heart
And I will shower you
With a love unspeakable.
I'll show you
The mysteries of this world.
Your heart's desires
Will be in alignment with Mine
Because you will know Me
Just as I know you.

Let it all go.

Will you marry Me?"

The Call

One day, her earth was rocked to the core
when she was first introduced to the love of The King.
The Holy Spirit spoke to her day and night
and her friends could never understand
why she began to go off by herself.
She was in the Presence of God,
for He had an extraordinary relationship with this girl,
one that the world was not ready to comprehend.
And the girl would listen
and talk back to Him in an unfamiliar tongue.
She was loved and she loved Him dearly.
The King called her to something special,
and she knew she would never be the same.

Wearing The Light: An Allegory

I woke up early
one Monday morning,
Looking forward to the brand
new day.

Thank You, Father
for waking me up.

Then I went into the bathroom
and looked at myself
in the mirror.

Who am I?

My reflection shone bright
and I couldn't see.
So I went into my
closet and dressed.
I put on Light.

As I walked out the front door
Creation greeted me
with a kiss and a soft hello,
"Good morning, Christ-Like."
Good morning, World.

I walked down the street
and people began to stare.
They were mumbling words
I couldn't hear.
I wonder why they are all
looking at me.

When I got to school
All of the other kids asked
and wondered,

"Something is different
about you."
"Why do you have so
much joy?"
"What is this new peace
on your face?"

When I was here last week
I didn't get a second
look from anyone.
What's different about me now?

"Good morning, Christ-Like."
Good morning, Professor.

"You seem to be getting
a lot of attention today."
It must be my new clothes.

"Yes, I see you're wearing
the new brand of Light."
I got it at church on Sunday.
The Pastor prayed over my life
and I exchanged my old clothes
for these new ones.

"Well it certainly does look
good on you."
Thank you, Sir.
People, even strangers,
are noticing me in
my new clothes.

"They may want some too."
Yes, well if they would like some
all they have to do is ask.

These clothes are not
just for me.
They were designed for all
people to wear.

"Yes, I believe you are correct,
Christ-Like.
You should look into getting
some of this Light for your family,
and then for your friends,
maybe even people
you don't know."

I'm hoping I can share this new
brand with my family and friends,
that I would help
to spread it worldwide.
These are the best clothes
I've ever had
and I will never throw them out.
There is a lifetime warranty,
ya know?

"Well isn't that a blessing."
Thank you for encouraging me,
Professor.
I feel that I have
been strengthened
to be bold enough to talk to
others about my new clothes,
rather than just letting them
stare and whisper.
I might as well share my story
of this divine exchange.

Pastor Barbara, My Gardener

She is as a faithful gardener
with a beautiful plot of land in her home.
Every morning she goes out
and walks in the midst of her joy,
watering, and pruning,
and sowing good seeds into the soil.
She knows every plant by name,
and cares for each flower according to its kind.
She is the only one with a heart like hers,
one that continuously seeks to keep her portion
healthy and developing.
Her garden surpasses all others in her neighborhood
because of the special attention to detail she maintains;
the unique seeds she uses,
the perfect amount of water she pours,
the beautiful hymns she sings to her florae
which helps them flourish even stronger,
and become more gorgeous
than any typical arrangement.
She is a stunning gardener
who speaks life into her own.
Others walk past her home
and watch her move about with such ease.
They wonder what makes her so distinctive,
why is her garden more abounding? More glorious?
Why they can't seem to get their sunflowers
to bloom in the harvest?
And how come their olive trees are without anointing?
The light always seems
to shine brightly above her garden
and the surrounding people are drawn to her spirit.
This beautiful gardener is fruitful in her labor
because she receives her special anointing
from The Lord who formed and fashioned her
with the same wisdom,
the same creativity,

and the same attention to detail
that she relies on to cultivate her garden.
This beautiful garden is full of gospel
and is a life center to light and love
where her precious plants and flowers
are nurtured to the point
where they can now blossom on their own.

Oh Jerusalem

The little girl woke up
speaking in a
language unknown.
Her own was Hebrew,
but this tongue she knew not.
She woke up
and there was a bright light
illuminating her room.

"I have chosen you.
Do not be afraid.
They will fear you,
but I am with you
to protect you
and to guide you."

She spoke to Him
in this new language
for the rest of the night
as He took this time
to build up her faith.

The next day
she spoke to her mother
of the wonders of the night.

"Shh, don't speak of this again.
They will condemn you
and put our family to shame,
just like they did Him,"
her mother claimed.

"Who is *Him*, mother?"

"The Christ, our Savior.
But no one must know
that we believe in the
Son of God the Most High."

"He spoke to me last night.
He is real."

"The world calls Him prophet
but we call Him Messiah."

"I want to share with everyone
my new language,
for it came to me in my sleep."

"It is the Spirit, daughter.
You are blessed
and you will be seated
in heavenly places,
but for now you must
keep it to yourself
or they will take you away."

"But He said to trust in Him,
that He is with me
and I believe Him, mother.
Why don't you?"

"Oh Jerusalem,
condemn not your child.
The small children
whose hearts are turned
towards Christ.
Spare them the persecution
and allow them
to follow Him in peace.
And for my daughter,
allow her to live a life

in the glory of our King.
You turned Him away,
but she has drawn close.

Oh Jerusalem,
It's time to wake up.
My child is shouting
from the rooftops,
and you turn the other way,
and continue to
walk in darkness.
But we will all perish
if our sins are not forgiven.
We must repent and turn
from the ways of our fathers.
My daughter is right,
she should not have to hide
her faith in the market.
She should not have to pretend
to be someone she is not.
And neither should we.

Oh Jerusalem,
the time is coming
where we need to reckon
with the sins of our fathers.
We can no longer
believe the lies,
but must admit the truth
and accept the Savior.
For through the eyes of my child,
I have seen His glory.
He is the Messiah,
the One we've been waiting for,
and He is calling to us,
yet we turn a deaf ear.
Open your eyes
and unharden your hearts
to the love of our God.
Take not my child from me.
as she continues to walk
in His ways,
speaking in tongues,
dreaming dreams and
having visions.
Condemn her not
like you did Jesus Christ,
but turn to the Lord
with your hearts wide open.
Seek Him as a child
through eyes of wonder."

Wake Up Call

This is a wake up call
For the sons and daughters
To rise to your calling
The time is coming
And your alarm is set for now
Arise and stand

This is a wake up call
For all you sleepers
And dreamers
And watchmen
Go to your post
Because the time is coming
And you need to be ready

Wake up
Wake up

This is a wake up call
To the apostles, the prophets
The evangelists and pastors
The teachers, all you leaders
It's time to operate
In your office
The harvest is ready
And the laborers
Must be serving

This is a wake up call
For the singers and dancers
The writers and artists
It's time to use your creativity
For the world is in danger
And your gifts are light

Wake up
Wake up

This is a wake up call
To those sitting in the pews
It's time to come
From the background
To move to the frontline
To be equipped for battle

This is a wake up call
For the worshippers
The time is coming
For those to worship
In spirit and truth
The prayer warriors
Come to the altar
It's almost time
And we need
All the children of God ready

This is a wake up call
The time is coming
When all God's children
Will be called to fight
Not one will be left out
Of this war
All hands on deck
From the youngest to the oldest

So wake up
Wake up
And rise to your calling.

Journal Reflection

Take some time to identify what your gifts are and what you are passionate about. Then reflect and record what you believe God has called you to do with the gifts and passions He has given you.

How can you begin today to share your faith with others through your gifts and passions so they can also know about the love of God and how He has transformed your life?

THE RESISTANCE

it's raining
all around me.
I skip in-between the
drops
and they miss me,
kissing the wind.

Strength & Freedom

I've been strong for too long,
carrying my own weight,
all the while walking through the mud
and in the rain.
The storm's been threatening to push me back
and throw me down,
but I've been strong.
I've never given up or given in.
Even when I was at my weakest point,
wanting to throw it all off of me and be free.
But my concept of freedom was wrong.
It was a liberty leading to death rather than life.
Because He already made a way
to take that pressure off of my back.
He lived and died and came back to life
to carry me through the storm,
in the mud, and the rain.
He is strong for me in my weakness.
I was never meant to carry my own weight,
not in this way.
And my freedom is to be found
in Christ who is my strength.
He is who He is,
so that I can find my freedom in Him.

The Resistance

I looked up,
and saw my hands covered in earth.
I was looking for something.
It had been lost,
and I couldn't find it.
Something was blocking my sight,
my path-
Sin.

The dirt on my hands was blood red.
All through the valley
I could see the dry bones of people lost,
their lives crying out from the ground-
Death.

I was to save them,
but I had lost my way.
I had wrapped myself in deception
and lies
and forgot my purpose.

I was searching for something,
and I found it in the enemy's arms.
Cradled so gently
that I didn't even know
he was carrying me to hell.
We had become one.
I lost my sense of self,
the son I was created to be.

I was lost
wanting to be found.
I was running to something
not knowing that I was running away
from the very One that I wanted,
and desperately needed.

And so I found myself
on the outside of myself
digging through this filth and mud
looking for something,
anything that would save me
from the guilt of the deaths
that I had caused,
and the fatality that was my life.
The empty body that I reside in.
I searched in the wrong places to be filled.
I long to be filled.
To be clean.

As I continued digging,
the clouds that had darkened the sky
began to subside.
A light more glorious than the sun
shared its warmth with me,
filling me with a heat
that restored these dry bones.
I didn't know what was happening.
Why I felt emotion in places
where coldness etched it's way
all the way to my core.
Life began to rebirth within me
the way a flower grows
in the field in springtime.
And the breath of life rushed into me
like the wind.
My hands were no longer covered in blood,
but washed clean.

And I looked up.

Could You Imagine, The Gift

At birth I was given a gift.
This gift was to carry the weight of the world's sins
and burdens in my own life.
At first this gift was light,
but as I grew up the weight grew heavier,
and I wanted to cast it all into the sea.
I didn't want it anymore,
but my father told me that I was special.
That if I didn't carry this weight,
all people would perish.
I was the only one strong enough to carry it all.
It was part of my purpose.
So I continued to walk with this weight.
My friends turned away from me.
My family disowned me.
People cursed at me, beat me,
and almost killed me.
They believed my gift was a curse,
and wanted nothing to do with me.
If only they knew that my gift was saving them,
then maybe they would love me
just like my father loves them.
Maybe their weight would lighten in me.
If they put their faith in him,
everything would be so much better
because this weight is heavy
and I don't know how much more I can bear-
being made an outcast
when I simply want to save the world.
But who else can possess this gift if not me?
I feel like I am being crushed
beneath a mountain of rocks.
My lungs are collapsing
as if I was drowning in the ocean,
and the pain burns like fire
consuming me into nothing.

Father, is there any other way
for your people to receive this gift?

Could you imagine?

Dreaming In The Light

"It shall be as when a hungry man dreams that he is eating,
but he wakens with his craving not satisfied; or as
when a thirsty man dreams that he is drinking,
but he wakens and is faint, and his thirst is not quenched."
-Isaiah 29:8 (AMPC)

I envision myself dreaming in the light,
but awakening to find darkness all around me;
searching for the one thing
that can quench my thirst and fill my hunger.
I am awake but my eyes are still shut.
Still unsure if I should accept
God's unconditional love for me,
allowing myself to become completely vulnerable
to Him and the desires He has for me.
I dreamed of good things to come while I was asleep,
but when I woke up those dreams did not come alive.

What am I doing?

What do I want?

What do I actually need?

My cravings are not satisfied.
I am not satisfied with where I am at the moment-

Physically
Emotionally
Mentally
Spiritually

I am not satisfied with my light remaining at
the same level of brightness it was
when I first got saved,

or having only dimmed since then.

I am not satisfied with being fed at church
every Sunday
and then spiritually starved the rest of the week.

I am not satisfied with having beautiful dreams
while I sleep
and then waking up to the mundaneness of life.

I am not satisfied with cultures current desire
to accept everything as permissible
when we know that everything is not beneficial.

I am not satisfied that I allow myself to walk in darkness
although I know my Savior in heaven
is the light of the world,
and He calls me to be light like Him.

"And afterward I will pour out My Spirit upon all flesh;
and your sons and your daughters shall prophesy,
your old men shall dream dreams,
your young men shall see visions."
-Joel 2:28 (AMPC)

I want to prophecy.

I want to dream dreams
and watch them come to life.

I want to see visions of peace in the world,
visions of heaven!

I want to live in the light,
and I will not be satisfied until I do.

Weight

The weight of the word "wait"
is beginning to fall on me.
I have been in this season of *waiting*
for some time now.
I feel like I may have reached the peak,
the highest point of this hike,
and the heaviness of this word
is starting to press down on me.
As I reach this difficult altitude,
I can begin to feel the pressure
restrain me from my upward climb,
and I just want to sink into the depths
rather than having to endure anymore.
I want to do Your will
and I want to press forward
with patient endurance,
but the weight of my wait is just so heavy.
I don't know how much longer I can stand it.
Being in this state,
on this plateau...
When will Your promises come to me,
oh Lord?
When will my faith be rewarded?
I feel like the Psalmist,
pouring out my soul to You,
hoping that You would hear my cry,
and remove this wait from my life.

Journal Reflection

Describe what you think about this first section of poems. What thoughts and emotions were elicited from reading them?

After reading *Part I, Before The Rain Began to Fall*, how do you feel about your personal relationship with God? Are you satisfied with where you are in your walk? Do you desire more? Write down why you are satisfied or why not and how you would like to grow if you want more.

PART II

THE RAIN IS FALLING

THE CHASE

the sun had chased me
across the face of the deep
knowing I would drown

feet got wet
letting go of myself
complete freedom
brave enough to jump
literally falling in love with Jesus
all I see is endless ocean

My Refuge Part Two- The Bench

In the early twilight,
we meet-
My Refuge.

I sit on the park bench,
secretly waiting for Your arrival.
I didn't have much time to prepare
so my hair is all over the place,
but I'm ready
and I'm waiting for Your voice
to speak with me.
Oh how I love Your voice.
It soothes all my fears
and calms my beating heart.
It's the best sound
in heaven and earth.
You amaze me when we meet,
telling me different things,
and listening to me.
I try not to bore You,
but You listen anyways.
You listen intently,
as if I'm the only girl in the world.
In these stolen moments
between us,
I imagine what it would be like
to run away with You
to a magical place
far, far away,
but You remind me
I have a purpose.
I must complete Your design.
That's why I'm here;
To love You,
and to do Your will.

Yes,
this is why we meet.
I finally understand.
You share Your love with me
with sweet kisses
and still words.
A love that I might share
with others
with the fierceness of a lion
and gentleness of You.

Holy Spirit,
I will wait for You
alone on this park bench
as ready as I can be
for Your arrival.
It fills me with joy,
our little love affair...

In the early twilight,
we meet-
My Refuge.

Childlike Love

go back to your first love
first love
with white roses
godiva chocolate
and scented candles
You painted the sky
my favorite colors
and laid the ocean
at my feet
the smell of fresh seawater
and the aroma of sage
fresh peppers
and basil
a feast prepared for
a princess
me, Your daughter
You spoil me
with Your grace and mercy
I am undeserving
yet forgiven
selfish innately
but redeemed
afraid but loved
the stars dance
for me at night
because You know the joy
I receive in my heart
when I decide to look up
mangoes
strawberries
pomegranates all for me
if only I would say yes
more than no
if only I would do
more than just say
to be more like You
You still love me
and show me
with the sunrise in the dawn
the cherry blossoms
in the spring
You watch me
and protect me
I love you, still
when I was a child
running free
with bouts of loneliness
anger
and fear
You were there
to hold my hand
playing with me
being light
I want to be light as air
light in the darkness
light like You
You held me close
and we danced
I could feel
Your warm embrace
the peace surrounding me
and filling me with
Your presence
my favorite things
we always did together
the pages of Your Book
opened itself to me
and breathed into me
page by page
word by word
my heart fell deeper
in love with You
for You loved me first
and You chased me
like a silly schoolboy
with a crush
will you be mine?
yes
no
maybe…

The Chase

I still wonder why **You** chased me.
Why **You** continued pursuit
after I pushed **You** away.
You continued after me
as if letting me go
would be the hardest thing.
Why didn't **You** want me to be *free*?
Did **You** love me?

I still wonder why you didn't chase **Me**.
Why you wanted to run *free*
into the wild lilies of the field.
I looked back
and you had turned yours,
walking away from **Me**.
My love-
why didn't you seek after **Me**?

You set me *free*.
Like a butterfly
I chose to go out into the wild
to roam, to spread my wings,
to fly.
But,
I was alone.

You are free in **Me**.
Come back.

I Love You, Eternally

Your love for me is so beautiful.
I couldn't imagine life without You.
I never want to be in anyone's arms but Yours.
The way You hold me,
and the way You kiss me softly-
It is like dancing in the rain with You,
like enjoying ice cream
on a beautiful summer day.

There is no end to Your love for me.
It carries me each and everyday,
extends its reach to those around me.
Your love for me is so sweet.
On the surface it is so simple,
but the sacrifice You made for me,
all to love me-

Is more than the human mind can fathom.
You make Your love known to me.
It called to me when I was a child.
It chooses me.
Never does Your love leave my side,
my front,
my back.

Your love is like an ocean
surrounding and filling me.
It overflows and I am able to love You,
I am able to love others.
Your love never leaves me wanting more,
it satisfies my soul,
it makes me smile without knowing.

How could anyone ever deny Your love?
Soften their hearts to receive it
for this is the greatest love-
the best love in the world.

No one should be without.
I am so thankful for Your love-
Your love for me is so beautiful.

I love you, eternally.

To Have And To Hold

She stood hopeful.
Waiting arm's length across from her groom-
Dashing as he was, calm as the wind.

Bride, do you take Eternity
To be your lawfully wedded husband?
To have and to hold,
To be your partner in life and one true love,
Cherishing His friendship and vowing to love Him
Today, tomorrow, and forever?

I do.

I now pronounce you, husband and wife.
Bride, you may now kiss Eternity.

Eternity held His Bridegroom close.
Fresh thyme and lavender from Bride's perfume,
Intertwined with the smell of incense
That was the very essence of Eternity.

The rest of the evening went accordingly-
The pair gracefully entered the reception.
A toast was made.
They shared their first dance.
Family and friends who were gathered together
Rejoiced in their glorious union.
Finally, Bride had made a commitment to Eternity.
She was His joy and He was her peace.
He passionately pursued her for years
Before she finally had the courage to say yes.
Or maybe she was finally exhausted of World-
Beautiful, yet deceptive in his ways.
She let go.

And to her surprise,
The ceremony was better
Than she could have ever imagined.
The reception, perfect-
A heavenly celebration of love.

For Bride and Eternity, life was just about to begin.

Journal Reflection

After reading these poems in *The Chase*, what are your thoughts on them? Which was your favorite poem and why?

What is your love story with God? Write a poem or short story of how you and Him met. What was it like when He called you to Himself? Utilize your five senses (touch, taste, smell, sight, and hearing) to describe your encounter with Him and if you have the opportunity, share what you have written with someone else.

THE SPARK

We seek Your face in the ashes
Beneath the rubble of the city
You still remain
Pure
Holy
Our Father who art in heaven
Hallowed be thy Name
For You reign all the days
Heaven and earth shall pass away
But You-
You still remain.

Rise Of The Sleepers

They have been hidden for so long that
no one can even tell the year or age
at which they fell asleep.
Only a few out of the masses stayed awake.
Some attempted to continue living life
ordinarily every day,
while a handful were vigilant
as the others continued drifting off
into a wakeless existence.

Then there was a loud sound in the sky.
The curtain was being ripped apart.
The watchful were ready
and only those of the sleepers
that are in Him could perceive it.
They rose and began wiping
the sleep from their eyes.

The Ends Of The Earth

I was walking towards the edge of a cliff
until I suddenly stopped.
My feet were blistered.
My hands were trembling.
I had been walking for so long.

Where am I going?
What is the purpose of all this?
Why did I stop walking?
All of these questions were running through my head.

As I stood there, waiting to fall,
I felt my feet form into roots of a tree
and implant themselves into the ground.
There was no pain,
just cool earth surrounding my feet
and steadying my body
so the wind wouldn't push me off the edge.

Then the sky, like glass, began to crack
and there were horses
emerging rapidly from this newly formed seam:
a black one,
a red one,
a white one,
a pale green one.
The horses were on fire, but they weren't consumed.
I began to tremble, trying to run away
but my feet were engrained so deep in the ground,
all I could do was cover my eyes.
The sky turned light grey.
Although my eyes were closed,
the brightness seeped through my eyelids,
forcing tears to reopen them.

"It's time, go!"
I heard a voice cry out in a whisper,
but loud like thunder.

My senses were beginning to confuse me.
At once, the four horses each went in a different direction:
North.
South.
East.
West.

Where are they going?
Why am I here?

"You were on your way to death. I saved you."

Who are you?
My mouth was shut,
lips unmoved,
but I was heard from the voice above.

"You knew Me once before,
but you forgot your first love.
I need you to come back.
It's time."

Time for what?
I don't understand.
What is going on?

"I've sent My angels ahead of you.
I need you to go now.
I've established you in Me-
Your foundation has been set."

I stood, silent in mind and speech.

"You were sleeping.
Don't you understand now?
It's time to wake up.
I need you to save the world."

Me?
Save the world?
How can I?
I don't even remember my name.

"Your name is Son of the Almighty God.
The world is dying
and I need you to travel to the ends of the earth."

Am I dead?

"No.
You are alive in Me."

My mind was racing.
I saw images of my past
flash like a kaleidoscope before my eyes.
Then, as if I were dreaming,
I saw myself standing in the middle of the land.
It was soundless and I felt like air,
but all around me
I saw people crawling on the ground with
despair in their eyes.
They were coming towards me.

"You have to save them."

Instantly, my attention was focused in another place.

This time,
I was sitting in the middle of a grassy meadow.
I saw stunning colors that have no earthly name,
smelled sweet fragrances,
and was overwhelmed by peace.

What is this place?

"This will be your new home.
Finish the task I have set before you."

Once again I saw vibrant visions inside my head.
It was me in the future
and there was great destruction.
I was the only person walking in light.

"You have to save them."

When these vivid images that infiltrated my thoughts
came to an end,
I found myself back on the edge of the cliff
where I had been walking towards my death.
My feet were no longer rooted in the ground.
I was clothed in white,
wearing armor like a warrior.

I held a Bible in my right hand, written in Hebrew.
I can't read this.

"I will open your eyes."

In my left hand, I held a sword.
I can't fight.

"I will fight for you."

I don't know where I am going.

"I will lead you."

I am not adequate enough for this mission.

"I will empower you with My Holy Spirit."

How can I trust you?

"Trust Me in the death I died for you on the cross.
I love you and I will never abandon you.
I will build your faith along the journey."

I immediately felt all fear leave my soul and body.

I trust You.

I turned away from the edge of the cliff,
away from death,
and began running towards the path set forth before me.
I ran to the ends of the earth…

The Spark

Everywhere I looked,
in each direction,
people were beginning to wake up-
to stand,
letting their restraints fall loose.
They had been in bondage since the fall of man.
The time had finally come.
The sound of the chains hitting the ground
was as an alarm raging in the morning.
An army was rising up.

WAKE UP!!!!

WAKE UP!!!!

A little boy shouted with all of his might.
He was the spark that lit the fire,
and that blaze spread like wildflowers
across the nations
to every corner of the earth.
The revival is upon us.

Dear Father, My Heart Hurts

Dear Father,
is Your heart hurting?
Because my heart is hurting.
And if I am Your daughter, created in Your image,
with a heart after Yours,
then Your heart has to be hurting too, right?
Because what I see happening in this world-
in this place that has been my home,
is hurting my heart.
What is happening, Father?
What am I supposed to do?
What do You want me to do, Father?
Because I am Your daughter,
and I want to do Your will.
I want to be a witness of Your love,
and draw more people closer to You.
So please, Father, tell me what to do.
Because everything that is happening
doesn't make any sense.
Sometimes I feel like I'm stuck,
standing still in time
as the earth continues to spin around me.
As people get involved
in different social justice efforts
and take action-
being present in these situations
that are presently occurring.
What do I do, Father?
How do I move from this state of complacency
and stillness
to be active in creation around me?
Please tell me, Father
because my heart is hurting,
so Your heart must be hurting too.
And I still don't know how
to make sense of all this pain.
I need You to tell me what to do.
How am I supposed to feel?
How do You feel?

And I hear Him saying, "just be love."

The Answer

This is a revival song
No more waiting for the rain to come
It's time to get down on your knees and pray

Press through
Press through

The rain is coming
The rain is coming

The healing rain is coming

Open up your Word
And be refreshed
As restoration overtakes our land.

Journal Reflection

In "Dear Father, My Heart Hurts," the author shares how sometimes she doesn't know what to do with everything going on in the world, all the pain and injustice, and God tells her to just be love, walking out that love on the earth. Are there any specific causes that you feel passionately about to get involved in, and what are some ways you can be an expression of God's love in this world filled with hurt?

Before moving on to the next section, take some time to think about what revival means to you. Whether you have prior knowledge or not, take five minutes to write down whatever comes to mind.

THE REVIVAL

Holy Spirit, come
Fire of God
Let it burn bright into the night
Fill me with Your Spirit, Lord
That I may shine brighter than the light

Hallelujah!
I feel the Spirit.

Rain

I can feel the cool grass beneath my toes.
The wind is calm and the night clear,
but then I sense it-
the refreshing drops of rain falling.
The stars pour a shower of water onto the earth,
washing away the filth and bringing new life-
a fresh anointing.
As I tilt my head back and stick my tongue out,
I can taste the sweetness of Your promise
baptizing me in Your Spirit,
and filling me with new joy,
new peace,
new love.
I am Yours, forever.
Thank You for the rain.

The Waters Of Your Grace

God,

Flood this place with the wave of Your grace
So that we may be saturated in Your Presence,
That our lives would be submerged under the depths,
And our souls would be filled with Your Spirit.

Fill us
Fill us
Fill us
Fill me up, oh God.

I want to be hidden beneath the waters of Your grace,
Forever going deeper in Your love,
Moving further and further away from the shore,
And closer to You as I seek Your face.
The glory,
And the beautiful compassion
That is found in the deepest of oceans
When we surrender ourselves to You
Is the desire of my heart.
Nothing else can satisfy me the way that You do.
I'm giving up all of myself for more of You, God.
You are lovely.
My prayer is that the natural wonders of water
Be a refreshing,
A cleansing,
Drawing all nations unto you, God.
For we are an unworthy people.
But because of the vastness of Your grace and love,
We are stunned, oh God,
And made right with You.

Fill us
Fill us
Fill us

Fill me up, oh God.

The Revival

I saw a little girl
standing on top of the ocean.
There was darkness surrounding her,
but her hair and her dress were pure white,
flowing as a calm wind blew.
She was singing
and the stars were dancing to her tune.
As the little girl sang,
people walked towards the sun,
towards the light.
Her music was bringing healing
to a nation that was in pain.

The little girl was me.

A Piece Of Me

I left a piece of me in the Philippines
as I floated on water
filled to the brim with salt
that held me afloat
staring into the sun
as fish swam underneath me
and thimble jellyfish pinched my skin
the scene was gorgeous
heaven's beauty shining down on this space
with mountains in viewpoint
as the ocean spread itself wide
I was feeling freedom
not afraid of the depths of the deep
excitedly I had jumped in
exploring the profundities beneath me
as I laid on my back
I continuously thanked God
for the beautiful moment in time
and upon returning to the beach
I continued to stay immersed
within the clear blue
along the shoreline
as sand pebbles exfoliated my toes
my feet desiring to lead me in deeper again
the rain began to fall so
I tilted my head up towards the sky
and began to sing
it's raining all around me
I can feel it it's the latter rain…
I brought memories from Belize
to this place in the Philippines
and danced in the rain
where the land met the sea
being baptized over and over and over again.

Fire & Glory

Rain down Your fire
Drown us in Your glory
Rain down Your fire
Drown us in Your glory

Rain down
Rain down
Rain down

Glory
Overwhelm us

Fire
Cleanse us

We want to be renewed

Rain down fire
Drown us in glory
Rain down fire
Drown us in glory

Saturate us, God
In this revival song.

Prayer, Our Gateway To Revival

Dear Father,
we come to You this day with joy in our hearts
and thankfulness on our lips.
Expecting a move from You,
we wait patiently.

As we look to the revival that is here,
we look back at Your daughters
who knew the meaning of prayer.
Prayer as a means of worship,
and worship as an act of faith.
Your unfailing love and grace
has brought us to this place.

Lord, help us to be like Hannah
who was without child.
Who stood in Your presence and prayed to You,
pouring out her soul and rejoicing in Your salvation.
Who was then blessed with a son
that she gave back to You.

Lord, help us to be like Anna
who was a widow after seven years of marriage.
Who did not leave Your temple,
worshipping with fasting and prayer day and night.
Who was then blessed to see the newborn Messiah.

Lord, help us be like the faithful woman
who was known to the world as a sinner.
Who anointed Your feet with precious oil,
wetting Your feet with her tears,
she wiped them with her hair and sweet kisses.
Whose faith saved her because she loved much.

We look to these women
and the example of Christ,
who prayed unceasingly.

Who devoted themselves to steadfast supplication.
Who were sincere and unwearied in their hope.

We will pray with our hearts fixed on You.
We will pray expecting a move from You.
We will pray until Your rain breaks through.

River Of Life

"On the last and greatest day of the festival, Jesus stood and said in a loud voice, 'Let anyone who is thirsty come to me and drink. Whoever believes in me, as Scripture has said, rivers of living water will flow from within them.'"
–John 7:37-38 (NIV)

I sit still as the rain begins to pour over me,
over, and over, and over.
It drowned me out,
so all that was left of me was the spirit within,
calming my soul
and making me whole again,
helping me gain a new revelation of the season at hand.
It was as if the heavens
had emptied out all of the floodwaters
that had been stored up for this moment of refreshing.
For this moment of cleansing.
For this moment of revival.
Our prayers had been answered
and the rain has finally come.

I sit in the stillness of Your presence,
allowing this overwhelming amount of rainwater
to drench my body.
As it quenches my once enduring thirst,
I am filled up Lord.
I am filled up with Your Spirit.
I am filled up like a river
that flows from the mountaintops of Mt. Zion
into the streams that caress themselves into the towns,
and gives refreshment to the dry and weary land
that has been parched for so long.
Everything that was once dead
has no choice but to revive.
And the people revive,
once searching in all the wrong places

for the One who gives life.
The river gives life to the people as it flows
clear as crystal.

Healing has been out poured from the heavens!

I sit still and wonder what it would be like
to dip my toes in this river of life
that dwells eternally in the hands of my Savior.
How I long to be in that place where
the beautiful rain would continuously pour over me,
over, and over, and over,
and satisfy my deepest desire to exist in Your will.
That this overflowing of Your outpouring
would revitalize my life, God.
That would resuscitate the nations, God.
That it would restore Your sons and daughters
who You've called out of darkness,
but who have slipped back into a cycle
of self-righteousness and pride.
That this river of life, God, would disrupt the status quo
and give people an urgency
that claims no more church as usual.
That reaches to the ends of the earth, God,
tugging on the hearts and the creativity of the people
You've so masterfully created,
so exquisitely in Your wisdom,
to invade Babylon with that same knowledge,
and insight, and excellence
You've etched into our being.
If only we would have the desire to make that choice, God,
and follow You as You lead.
That we would yearn for You
in yielded anticipation of Your glory.

And as I sit still while the rain pours over my head,

over, and over, and over,
as if I am submerged in the ocean.
In the depths of Your deep,
so vast that I lose myself
and find You.
I cling to You, God,
because there is no other life vest
that can keep me afloat.
Only You are real, God.
I know this when I see the rainbow in the sky
after Your clouds have graced us
with this abundance of life-giving water.
I know that You are real when I look into the atmosphere,
and it has been painted
different shades of blue, purple, pink and orange,
and the birds fly back home when they're supposed to,
and the flowers bloom in spring,
and the stars shine brighter
when the clouds have gone away.
You, God, told them to perform in this manner,
because they were fashioned with a purpose,
just like me, who You have called greater than these.
I know that You are real because
no other explanation
can give me peace about the creation of this world
other than knowing and believing that You are sovereign.

And I get peace like a river, when I read Your Word.
When I pray to You knowing that You hear me,
that You love me.
I long for all people to know
this deep and intimate tenderness,
praying that this thirst-quenching rain
will be a river of life
for those who thirst for You, Lord.
Because You are good.

And You fill us up so that we will never thirst again.
Who else can claim this of their god?
Who else can satisfy?
Who else can save?
Who else?

There is none like You in all the earth.
And as the rains fall in their season,
I will continue to sit still
and allow the waters of Your grace to wash over me,
over, and over, and over,
so that I will be abounding in Your love.
So that the river that lives within me will overflow
and give rest to the weary souls
who are aching for a manifestation of Your presence.
Your river will continue to flood throughout the nations
as more people receive Your Word,
and we will worship.
This life-giving water within me will never run dry
because You are the living water,
longing for Your people to be thankful for the rain.

We Are

Hear our earnest prayer, oh, God
and draw us closer to You.

Bring us to our knees
under the weight of Your magnificent glory
and strengthen us to stand back up, on fire for You.
Help us give ourselves completely to You, God.

Fill us.
We yearn for You.
Wake us up
and prepare us for the revival set before us.
We are Yours, oh, God.

We are the sons and daughters
who wait for Your rain to fall.

We will stand on the rock of our foundation,
renewing our mind through prayer
and reading of the Word
and choosing to serve Christ this day.

Worshipping and praying.
Interceding and healing.

In the name of Jesus,
we will ascend to our call
as the David's and Esther's of our generation.

Please hear our humble desires, oh, Lord.
In Your precious Name we pray,
Amen.

Journal Reflection

Take some time to pause, reflect, and pray about whatever may be on your heart right now. You can either pray out loud or write your prayers down. Just be open and honest with God during this time and then sit and wait for Him to respond. If He responds right away, write it down and remember this time that The Lord spoke to you.

THE BEGINNING

creation was formed
patient hearts search for the truth
wisdom falls like rain

fly higher than clouds
dreams of heaven abounding
we wait for beauty

I'm Letting Go

So we find ourselves in this space-
This awkward uncomfortableness
That makes itself cozy in the lives that we live.
And we are forced to accept
That things will never be the same.
That this season of growth
Is meant to stretch us beyond ourselves,
Creating in us new hopes and dreams
That will only come to light when we finally let go.

Changing Seasons

The leaves fall every fall
just like the snow
is expected to come in winter,
but the spring brings
uncertain hopes
and dreams.
We know the flowers will arrive,
but when they bloom,
will they hold out their splendor
until summer
when the heat threatens to
extinguish the beauty of the land?

What will come
when we let go of ourselves
and let God lead
every intention of good
that we have?
Leaving the bad in the past
and moving towards
an even brighter future-
His light.
How do we let go and
believe for this new season of life
with such confidence?

When will we know
that the promises made
will come to fruition?
Like the assurance of leaves
falling in fall,
or snow coming in winter,
and flowers blooming in spring,
and heat burning in summer.

How can we look forward to
the new seasons of our lives?
Does faith not have a face or a
picture in which we can
place our hope?
Just as the loveliness and majesties
of the seasons
in which we are able to witness
God's promises
physically and visually
able to touch, see, smell,
hear, and feel.

Yet our seasons are unseen,
they are unexpected,
but sometimes we can sense
when our time is near
to change,
to fall,
to bloom,
and to burn brighter
than the greatest lights
in this atmosphere.

We wait in hopeful expectation
that our seasons will be beautiful.
They will be different,
unlike the seasons
which forever remain the same.
We will be different.

If we only believe
in the beauty of our dreams
and the promises of our God.
Our fall will not die.
Our snow will not cover.
Our flowers will not wilt.
We will defy the odds of nature
because we are created

in His image.
We were created to be
infinitely stunning
despite the season of change.

We embrace our new seasons
with hope, joy, and peace,
knowing that the grace of God
will allow us to see Him
in every season.

The Year I Learned To Fly

There's a beautiful girl in the world
who always dreamed she would fly.
When the girl was a child,
her father gave her a blue kite
that she would play with after school.
The kite flew high, but not high enough.
When the girl became a teenager,
her best friend took her on a roller coaster ride
for the first time in her life.
The adrenaline rush was supreme,
but the coaster didn't fly far enough.
When the girl became an adult
she received a gift in the mail.

The note on the gift read-
"To my dearly beloved beautiful girl
today you are an adult.
Your whole life you've dreamed to fly
and the day is finally here.
I gave you the kite to see how high you would go.
The coaster ride we shared
was to tell what distance was best for you.
And now I give you these wings
so that you will no longer be held back.
You are able to go as high
and as far as your dreams will take you,
because I know you are now ready
to follow them completely.
Don't be afraid of the winds that may blow
or the storms that will come-
these wings were made to hold and protect you.
So fly high and fly far
and know that I'm right beside you."

And when she finally got her chance
to put on her wings and fly,

she soared higher than anyone could ever imagine
and farther than her eyes could see.
And this beautiful girl in the world
who always dreamed she would fly
defied all odds and flew into the sky.

A Beautiful Place In My Life

This place is beautiful.
I can't imagine being anywhere else.
Look at the flowers, how they bloom.
The way the sun glistens in the sky.

This place is beautiful.
My soul dances
and my heart leaps with joy.
The way I feel here with You-
indescribable.

This place is beautiful.
It's like heaven on earth.
Light has become life,
life has become love.
Peace and joy surround me.

This perfect place between You and me
is one I've been searching for all my life.
Thank You for bringing me here.
This beautiful place.

Haikus For John

The Foundation

A brave prince he lives
there is meaning in his name
God's grace and mercy.

The Question

The boy stood alone
until the day God came home
and life was now love.

The Call

Jumping high, wanting
to touch the sky and feel the
glorious embrace.

The Resistance

His light was bottled
fiercely exploding inside
created for earth.

The Chase

As a god he was
like the Spirit within him
tearing down giants.

The Spark

And he saw the star
explode brightly in the sky
awakening him.

The Revival

The revival came
swift and steady like the fox
his bow set to aim.

The Beginning

Prayers of a new world
he sang his song in the air
God, please send the rain.

The Beginning

Thank You for this fresh start, Father.
Just like the rain that fell this afternoon
and washed away the worries of the day,
Your grace has refreshed and revitalized me.
Giving me new energy
and new zeal to continue on this path
to what You have for my life.
Better is coming,
and I am committed to reaching beyond the sunset
that now glows past the clouds
and through my bedroom window.
You are so good, God.
And Your mercies endure forever.
I love You with all of my heart, Father
and I thank You for walking beside me on this journey.

Journal Reflection

After reading *Part II- The Rain Is Falling*, how have your thoughts shifted?

Reflect on seasons of change/growth that you have had to go through. With as much detail as possible, describe the current season of life that you are in and how it is changing you.

What are the dreams that God has placed inside of you? Take some time to write them down and dream with God. Don't allow your past experiences, current circumstances, or fears to hinder you from dreaming BIG and imagining the amazing plans He has in store for you! Write your vision down and discover what steps He wants you to take in order to fulfill those ideas.

PART III

AFTER THE RAIN HAS FALLEN

THE SEEKING

you look so beautiful
standing there
arms wide open
waiting for me to run into them
what a wonderful view
anticipating this moment
running to my love
running to you
don't let me go, okay?

I love.

After The Rain Has Fallen

Where do we go from here?
After the rain has fallen,
leaving the soil moist
and prepared for new growth.
After the horn has sounded
and the walls have all come down,
leaving us open and vulnerable.
What happens once the sleepwalkers
have risen to their call?
Have been awoken by the sound.
Have been changed by the Spirit.
We have reached the tipping point
and our defenses are ready to drop.
Our minds are being transformed,
our language is becoming more in tune
with the One who gave us life,
and our song is being heard in the heavens.
The revival was here
and we outshined all of our fears,
reaching towards the light-
the hope.
What do we do
now that we have felt the rain on our heads?
On the tips of our tongues.
We have tasted Your sweetness
and witnessed Your wonder,
and we want more, God.
More of You.
Everyday,
every moment of our lives, Father,
we want more.

And so, we will continue to seek Your face.

"For I know the plans and thoughts that I have for you," says the Lord. "Plans for peace and well-being and not for disaster to give you a future and a hope. Then you will call on Me and you will come and pray to Me, and I will hear [your voice] and I will listen to you. Then [with a deep longing] you will seek Me and require Me [as a vital necessity] and [you will] find Me when you search for Me with all your heart. I will be found by you," says the Lord. "and I will restore your fortunes and I will [free you...]"

–Jeremiah 29:11-14 (AMP)

I Love Thunderstorms

I love thunderstorms.
I love the sound of the rain hitting the pavement,
barefoot walks through the grass or on gravel
as the refreshing rain pours over me like a shower.

I love thunderstorms.
I love the roaring of thunder
as the lightning illuminates the sky,
being an expression of God's great power
and strength.

The rain falls,
washing over the land with restoration and healing,
bringing life on the inside,
seeping deep down within to heal old wounds.

Even when the rain seems cold and tiresome,
and the thunder and lightning are both loud and untimely,
it's always the perfect time
for the special silence that comes with noise.
You just have to listen closely.
It's the same as waiting for
the voice of the Holy Spirit to be clear
in a world filled with distractions.
He's always speaking to us,
but are we listening?

I love thunderstorms
because they allow me to sit quietly in my room,
watching God's handiwork in the sky above
and truly listen.

Freedom

Conversation in your soul
I know what freedom feels like

I know what freedom feels like
But I'm still apprehensive
Wanting to be comfortable
Being myself in Him
Can be uncomfortable

Still

I know what freedom feels like

I know what freedom feels like
Not this watered down tradition
We call religion
Where church attendance
Is more important
Than relationship
Personal
Deep in your soul
Spirit to spirit
Saving grace friendship
With Christ

Love

I know what freedom feels like

I know what freedom feels like
Not concerned
With the way man views me
With my words of
Encouragement
And mission trips
Not worried about
The separation
Only wishing to please
My Father in heaven

I know what freedom feels like

I know what freedom feels like
Better than Sunday
Morning brunch
Or sipping Champagne
With chocolate
Covered strawberries
More like forehead kisses
In the rain
Not scared that the water
Will mess up my natural hair

Freedom
In its purest form
And most like heaven on earth
That one could ever embrace
Is believing and
Living unashamed
In the beauty of Christ's love
I know what freedom feels like

I know what freedom is.

Before I Get There

I want to travel the world.
I want to see places and people
I've only imagined in my dreams.
I want to be curious and explore the wild unknown.
I want to touch lives
and be changed by the love and spirit
of the individuals and communities I come across.
I want to jump into bodies of water filled with sea-life.
I want to climb hills and mountains
that overlook breathtaking landscapes.
I want to run through fields of wildflowers
and meadows with grass taller than me.
I want to be kissed by dolphins,
and listen to the birds sing me sweet lullabies.
I want to leave a piece of me-
through my words, and through my touch,
and through my smile,
on every sacred place I stand.
I want to live a limitless life that exceeds
the outer limits of where my expectations lay.

I want to share a kiss with my husband,
my Love,
on top of the Eiffel Tower,
and standing under Angel Falls,
and at the top of Mt. Kilimanjaro,
and walking across the Great Wall of China,
and while we pick grapes in the valleys of Italy,
and as we are worshipping
amongst the believers in Jerusalem-

The Holy City,

Zion.

And when I reach the outer depths
of this beautiful earth that God created,

I will be sure to let my light shine so brightly
that I will leave a trace of heaven to cue the golden path
towards the One we've all been searching for in this world.

I will continue traveling until I return home
to the gracious garden where a marriage feast
is already prepared for me in eternity,
lavishly set and awaiting my arrival down the aisle
after my journey is completed.

And I know this will be home.
More real than this life,
more gorgeous than my mind could fathom,
and more wondrous than the seven wonders of the world.

And although my heart is drawn to seeing
everything glorious that this world has to offer,
my spirit is at rest knowing the One who created it all.

All for us to see, to inspire, to taste, to love, to believe.

Please Send More Rain

I was dreaming
and it was so vivid.
Everything within me
believed I was living my dream.
I looked up towards the sky,
captivated by the
speckles of light
that seeped through the clouds
lined with silver and purple hues.
The rain was on the verge
of exploding amidst
the heavens,
allowing its downpour
to soak through the soil
which had become dry,
without life
just like the people
that walked the earth-
He created it.
With one magical Word,
He spoke light and life
into a world covered
in darkness.

Light!

A word that is now taken so
lightly
that the blackness
has been able to penetrate
even the sunniest of places
and brightest of souls.

Light!

Is what we are in this place.
What we are
supposed to be in this place.

Light!

Has awoken me from my dream
and highlighted the new growth
in the land
from the rain that has fallen
on the moistened soil
that I now stand on-
bringing new life to this
foundation,
sprouting new hope
in this current situation.

Reviving!

Reviving!

Reviving!

Life that once before
yielded to the constant drought,
sin,
death,
that lurks in the darkness,
bringing back to life
those who have fallen asleep.

This *rain*-
This beautiful water falling
from the sky
is as refreshing as
the living water
welling up and overflowing
on the inside of the
hearts of those
who continually seek His face.

Yes

A refreshing revitalization of the land
and the spirit alike.

How I long to dance in this rain
with **you**
and celebrate the newness of faith
being built up in the believers.
Creating a space in our lives
for the promises
He so wishes to lavish upon us
generously.

This *rain*-
This sometimes inconvenience in life
has conveniently become
exactly what I needed to save my life.

Father, please send more rain.

10.8.16: My Revival

It's all coming full circle
This five-year journey that I've been on
I'm learning more and more about revival everyday
It's taken me some time to see
How God not only sends His fire and rain
To cleanse the whole earth
But to each and every child of God
Whose hearts are open to His love

It was a night unlike any other
Where I understood the yearnings of my spirit
How when our hearts are aligned with God's
His prayers fill our mouths
His joy becomes our own
He fills us with a passion
That extends His love beyond ourselves
We reach nations
Standing in one place
In one small church
In a city amongst many
And we are changed
I was changed

I was affirmed in my "Yes" to God
To His power to live and move through my being
And I was rewarded with the gift
Of understanding my calling
I was graciously given answers
To the questions I had been asking my whole life
What on earth am I here for?
What is my purpose in life?
What am I supposed to do with these gifts inside of me
That I never quite felt like have fully matured?
How do I get from where I am right now
To wherever I'm supposed to be in the future?

My prayers that night
Were for people across the nations to wake up
To rise up to their call
Little did I know that I was being awakened myself
That the covers were being pulled back
From my time asleep
And my mission made clear
I was captured by complete and utter joy
Laughing uncontrollably joy
Dancing
Singing
Praising
Shouting
Hallelujah to my God, the Most High God
It was a new day
My purpose was made known to me clear as day
And a messenger was sent
To confirm the words that I had been given
I knew that my life would never be the same
That my ministry is only just beginning
This was my revival

And then the testing came
Fire came
Trials of life came and almost forced me to believe
That I was incapable of fulfilling my purpose
But God
His Word came rushing back to me
Reminding me that He's been there too
He's been in the wilderness
He's done the fast
He's withstood the devil
And He gave us power to do the same
Jesus died so that we COULD do the same
So that we would always trust
And believe in His love for us
It's always been about His love

Through it all
The fire and the rain
We can see the silver lining
An eternity in paradise with Him
Forever
This is why we pray for revival
This is why we are to repent and turn from our sins
So that every man, woman, boy, and girl
Can experience the life-changing love of God
Through His Son Jesus Christ
Who died on the cross for our salvation
And live the beautiful life we were created for
In the sweet presence of the Holy Spirit
This is why we ask for the rain
So that our hearts will be transformed
Into good soil for fruit to grow and give life

I know the road ahead won't be easy
But I also know that He loves me
And He will never leave me
So I'm excited to see and experience
Everything that my Father has for me

And this is only the beginning...

"Now [emphasis added] grow in the grace and knowledge
of our Lord and Savior Jesus Christ.
To him be the glory both now and
to the day of eternity. Amen."
-2 Peter 3:18 (ESV)

About The Author

Raine K. Brandon loves to write and encourages people to communicate with God through journaling as a beneficial way to build an intimate relationship with Him. Her heart's desire is that this generation would turn their lives towards Jesus Christ, accept Him into their hearts, and seek Him with everything that's inside of them. Then people will learn more about the Father's love for them and the gifts He has placed inside of them in order to fully walk out the call of God on their life through the grace and power of the Holy Spirit.

She graduated with her Bachelor of Arts degree in Sociology from Hampton University and her Master's degree in Social Work from University of Maryland, Baltimore. Raine currently lives in Maryland with her husband John*. *Please Send More Rain* is her first published work.

For more information about this book and the author, email her at rainekbrandon@gmail.com or follow her on social media (Facebook, Twitter, and Instagram) @rainekbrandon.

**Raine and her husband John will be leaving their home state of Maryland to become new residents of Florida in 2018.*

71259428R00078

Made in the USA
Middletown, DE
21 April 2018